CRAZY CREEPY CRAWLERS

EXTRAORDINARY
INSECTS

Thanks to the creative team:
Senior Editor: Alice Peebles
Fact checking: Kate Mitchell
Designer: www.collaborate.agency

Hungry Tomato™
A division of Lerner Publishing Group, Inc.
241 First Avenue North
Minneapolis, MN 55401 USA

For reading levels and more information, look up
this title at www.lernerbooks.com.

Main body text set in Calisto MT 12/13.
Typeface provided by Monotype Typography.

Library of Congress Cataloging-in-Publication Data

Names: Turner, Matt, 1964– author. | Calle, Santiago, illustrator. |
Turner, Matt, 1964– Crazy creepy crawlers.
Title: Extraordinary insects / Matt Turner ; Santiago Calle,
illustrator.
Description: Minneapolis : Hungry Tomato, [2017] | Series: Crazy
creepy crawlers | Includes index.
Identifiers: LCCN 2016022391 (print) | LCCN 2016024499 (ebook)
| ISBN 9781512415568 (lb : alk. paper) | ISBN 9781512430790 (pb
: alk. paper) | ISBN 9781512427165 (eb pdf)
Subjects: LCSH: Insects—Juvenile literature.
Classification: LCC QL467.2 .T828 2017 (print) | LCC QL467.2
(ebook) | DDC 595.7—dc23

LC record available at https://lccn.loc.gov/2016022391

Manufactured in the United States of America
1-39916-21386-7/27/2016

CRAZY CREEPY CRAWLERS

EXTRAORDINARY INSECTS

By Matt Turner

Illustrated by Santiago Calle

HUNGRY TOMATO™

CONTENTS

EXTRAORDINARY INSECTS

We humans may think we rule the planet, but insects are pretty powerful too!

For a start, they outnumber us. There are roughly ten quintillion (10,000,000,000,000,000,000) insects alive at any one time, from more than 900,000 species. And they're far older than us, going back nearly 400 million years, long before the dinosaur age. They're about 120 million years older than the flowering plants too. In other words, flowering plants evolved to survive alongside existing insects, not the other way around.

Some insects live alone, but others such as ants, bees, and termites form complex societies, working together to build structures, gather food, nurse their young, and defeat enemies.

Modern insects have developed in some amazing ways, resulting in their exceptional beauty, camouflage, engineering skills, weapons, defenses, and sneaky survival tricks. They also affect humanity in ways that are both welcome and unwelcome. But the great thing about them is that you have an entire insect zoo in your home and yard. Go take a look!

GREAT SURVIVORS

Cockroaches first appeared about 320 million years ago. Modern-day roaches developed about 200 million years ago and walked with the dinosaurs.

A cockroach can live for weeks without its head. And the separated head can keep on waving its antennae for hours!

Cockroaches are scavengers. In a pinch they will eat just about anything: glue, grease, soap, wallpaper paste, leather, bookbindings, or even hair.

Some roaches are big. *Megaloblatta longipennis* has a 7-inch (17.8-centimeter) wingspan, and the Australian rhino cockroach is the world's heaviest.

Cockroaches are fast! Once all six legs are in motion, a roach can sprint at speeds of up to 5 feet (1.5 meters) per second. And they're elusive, too, with the ability to "turn on a dime" while in full stride.

COCKROACHES

Flick on the kitchen light at night, and you may see a flat brown insect racing over the floor to a dark hiding place. Few insects are so unloved as the cockroach—but, of about 4,600 known species, only thirty or so are pests. Some are specially adapted for cold or dry habitats, but most are generalized eat-anything, go-anywhere critters . . . which helps explain how roaches are found in almost every corner of the planet.

MADAGASCAR HISSING COCKROACH
GROMPHADORHINA PORTENTOSA
Size: up to 3 inches (76 millimeters)
Lifespan: 2–5 years

NUCLEAR PROOF
In a nuclear attack, among the survivors would be fruit flies and cockroaches. They can handle doses of radiation that would kill humans.

SWEET TOOTH
If a cockroach is introduced to a sweet taste such as vanilla or peppermint, it will drool in anticipation when it later detects the scent in the air.

Working Together

Worker ants of all sizes work together. *Left:* An *Atta* major carries a leaf fragment, giving minors a ride. In return, they guard her from parasitic flies. *Center:* A *Pheidologeton* supermajor acts as a troop transport for minors. *Right:* An army worker grooms a soldier's jaws.

A weaver ant gently holds a larva and taps it with its antennae to make it release silk. The ant uses the silk to stick leaves together and build a home.

A queen driver ant is so big—up to 2 inches (5 cm) long—that her tiny workers, just one-tenth her size, have to push her around.

Some workers in carpenter ant colonies take defense to the extreme. When attacked, they explode, blasting toxic gunk all over their enemies.

Honeypot ant workers, or repletes, hang from the ceiling of the nest and regurgitate liquid sugar and protein from their abdomens to feed the other ants.

ANTS

Ants are found worldwide, having evolved only about 130 million years ago from ancient wasps. They form colonies, sometimes millions strong, made up of several castes—queen, workers, soldiers, and so on—all performing different roles. They work together to build the nest, raise the young, and fend off enemies. Ants will fight to the death for the colony's survival.

AUSTRALIAN BULLDOG ANT
MYRMECIA BREVINODA
Size: worker 0.7–1 inch (17–26 mm)
Lifespan: up to 2 years

FIERCE
A bulldog ant is so fierce that, if it is cut in two, its head will still try to bite its abdomen, and the abdomen will sting the head.

HEAVY
If you took a giant set of scales to the Brazilian Amazon rain forest and put all the ants on one side and all of the other land vertebrates (mammals, birds, reptiles, and amphibians) on the other, the ants would be four times heavier.

Fearsome Larvae

This is an egg-cellent spot.

Antlions are holometabolous: they go through a complete egg-larva-pupa-adult life cycle. First, a female lacewing deposits eggs in dirt or sand.

Neat sandpit!

The hatched larva digs a cone-shaped pit, burying itself at the bottom, but leaving its long, toothed jaws free. Then it lies in wait.

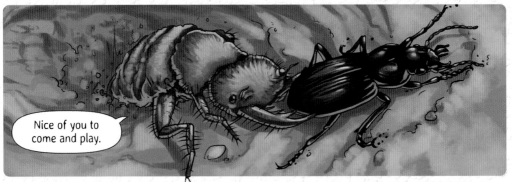

Nice of you to come and play.

If prey tumbles in, the antlion may flick sand up to cause a sandslide, knocking the victim off its feet. Bursting out from its hiding place, the antlion uses the hollow teeth of its jaws first to inject its victim with digestive venom, then to suck out the resulting "soup," leaving nothing but an empty husk.

You might call this the boring bit.

The larva pupates inside a round cocoon about the size of a chickpea. It may remain here, buried in sand, for several years.

I waited three years . . . for this?!

Finally, the long, winged adult hatches. It spends the next few weeks searching for a mate and not feeding. Its adult life lasts only about one month.

ANTLIONS

Antlions are not ants but lacewings, and there are about two thousand species found worldwide. While the adult is a winged insect that looks like a rather scrawny dragonfly, the larva is a more fearsome beast. And while sometimes it simply hides among leaves or in rock cracks, it is best known for its habit of digging a pit in the sand, where it lurks with jaws gaping wide, waiting to capture prey and suck it dry.

ANTLION
MYRMELEON SP.
Size: larva up to 0.6 inches (15 mm)
adult up to 3.1 inches (80 mm)
Lifespan: larva 3 years or more
adult 25–45 days

SNEAKY
The name antlion is centuries old. Maurus, a medieval scholar, said of the larva that "it conceals itself in dust and kills ants that carry provisions."

NICKNAME
Some Americans call antlions doodlebugs. In *Tom Sawyer*, the classic tale by Mark Twain, Tom talks to a doodlebug to coax it out of its hole.

Borers and Battlers

These are male giraffe weevils (*Lasiorhynchus barbicornis*) from New Zealand. They look rather different from the Madagascar giraffe weevil opposite, but they probably fight the same "snout battles" to decide who mates with females. Their huge snouts measure up to half the male's total length of 3 inches (8 cm).

In the acorn weevil it's the female who has the longer snout. She uses it to bore a hole in an acorn, then turns around and lays an egg in it.

The larva develops inside the acorn, then drills its way out and drops into the soil, where it pupates for a year or two before becoming an adult.

The palm weevil lays up to five hundred eggs at a time in coconut, date, and oil palms. Its big larvae chew through the timber, ruining the crops.

Insects are rich in protein. In Malaysia, people cook weevils in a dish called Sago Delight. In Vietnam, weevils dipped in fish sauce are eaten alive. Mmm!

WEEVILS

Weevils are smallish beetles, usually with a long snout, and their antennae have an "elbow" joint. There are over 60,000 known species, and although farmers hate them because they burrow into plants and damage crops, weevils have some fascinating adaptations. In some species, the snout—or rostrum—reaches extraordinary lengths, and males use theirs to battle each other over females.

MADAGASCAR GIRAFFE WEEVIL

TRACHELOPHORUS GIRAFFA

Size: up to 1 inch (25 mm)
Lifespan: 1 year

QUANTITY
Nearly one in four of all life forms is a beetle, and of these, around one in five is a weevil. Beetles are everywhere!

WELL-NAMED
The male Madagascar giraffe weevil is nearly all neck! After mating, the female (which has a much shorter neck) carefully lays her eggs in rolled-up leaves, one egg per leaf.

INCREDIBLE HULKS

Giant weta regularly weigh 1.2 ounces (35 grams), more than a mouse. The heaviest on record—a pregnant female—weighed in at 2.5 ounces (70 g).

Like her cousins the crickets, the female weta has a spiked ovipositor, which she uses for laying eggs. She pushes the eggs into damp soil.

The mountain weta lives high above the snowline. It can survive being frozen stiff! It just thaws out in warmer weather and carries on.

Tusked weta were discovered in 1970. Males use their tusks in jousting battles over females and rub them together to make a rasping noise.

Cave weta aren't giants, but they do have long legs that can span up to 8 inches (21 cm) on a body just 1.4 inches (3.5 cm) long. You can find lots of them clinging to the roofs of cool, damp caves in New Zealand, so if you go looking for them, remember to check your coat collar afterward! They're good at jumping too.

GIANT WETA

A flightless vegetarian with a face like a samurai warrior, armed with powerful jaws and spiky legs . . . and heavier than a sparrow? Meet the giant weta! All eleven species live in New Zealand, where introduced predators have wiped out their mainland populations, leaving the only survivors on islands or reserves. There are smaller weta species too, living in caves, forests, and mountains.

GIANT WETA
GENUS: *DEINACRIDA*
Size: up to 4 inches (10 cm)
Lifespan: 2 years

ISLAND GIANTS
Giant weta are examples of island gigantism: animals or plants that evolve in isolation on islands can, over time, become enormous.

UGLY
The Maori people of New Zealand named this insect *wetapunga,* after the god of ugly things, or *taipo,* meaning "ghost" or "spook."

LEAF LOOKALIKES

Antonio Pigafetta found leaf insects when he explored the Philippines in 1519–1522. He thought they were "walking leaves" that fed on air.

Nymphs (young) shed their skin several times as they grow. If they lose a leg or antenna, they can regrow it—the limb gets bigger with each molt.

Phasmids have amazing night vision. With each molt, their eyes grow bigger and more sensitive. So while nymphs come out by day, adults are mostly nocturnal.

Some leaf insects spray a defensive fluid from glands in their necks to keep predators away. It's very painful if it gets in the eyes.

Relatives of the leaf insects include the two-striped walkingstick or "devil rider," an American species. The male and female are usually found attached together in summer and fall when mating. They go everywhere together, and they don't separate until one of the pair dies and drops off!

LEAF INSECTS

Leaf insects or "walking leaves" have taken camouflage to the extreme, with bodies that have evolved to look exactly like real leaves. They have veins and ribs, and even crinkly brown edges. Related to stick insects, they are known as phasmids. Like some wasp species, female leaf insects can produce eggs without the help of a male, and the eggs hatch into more females!

GIANT LEAF INSECT
PHYLLIUM GIGANTEUM
Size: up to 4 inches (11 cm)
Lifespan: 5–7 months

RARE MALE
There are male leaf insects, but they're incredibly rare. The first male giant leaf insect was only discovered as late as 1994.

CANNIBAL
Stick insects make great pets. But if they run out of leaves to eat, they'll eat leaf insects instead . . . so you can't keep the two together in one cage!

Cool Camouflage

The mantis is the only insect able to move its head 180 degrees around each way. So it can sit completely still and keep carefully watching prey.

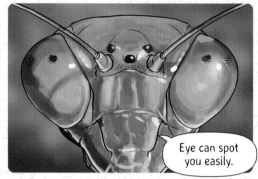

The two dots that float around the eyes are false pupils. These parts of the eye are an optical illusion and appear black because they are absorbing light.

Like leaf insects, mantises walk in a wobbly way. They do this for an extra camouflage effect, swaying like a twig in a breeze. The flower mantis on the left, however, is putting on a deimatic display—a startling move that shows off its bright colors. It sometimes does this to scare off predators.

Insect camouflage reaches beautiful extremes in species such as the orchid mantis. They're hard to pick out from the flowers on which they lurk!

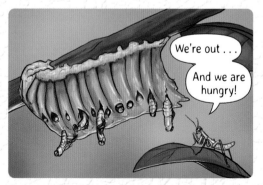

The mantis egg sac, or ootheca, looks like a squeeze of toothpaste. Newly hatched nymphs look just like mini mantises.

MANTISES

The mantis is an ambush expert, a predator so well-camouflaged that it melts into the scenery when perched on a plant. Its big compound eyes watch for movement, and if another insect settles near, the mantis flicks out its long, spiked forelegs to snatch it. The different species show variations of camouflage—some look like colorful flowers while others resemble rotten leaves or dry twigs.

VIOLIN MANTIS
GONGYLUS GONGYLODES
Size: female 4 inches (10 cm),
male 3-3.5 inches (8–9 cm)
Lifespan: 1 year,
sometimes 2

THORNY
The violin mantis has an extra-long thorax, which resembles the slender neck of a violin. It also looks just like the dry twigs of rose bushes, where it likes to hide.

VANISHING ACT
A young mantis may change color—from brown to green, say—when molting, in order to blend more closely with its environment.

GLOWING IN THE DARK

A male *Photinus* firefly flashes a special pattern to attract a female of the same species. She then flashes an answer that leads him to her.

Sometimes, a sneaky female from the genus *Photuris* tricks a *Photinus* male by flashing the correct answer . . . and then eats him when he finds her!

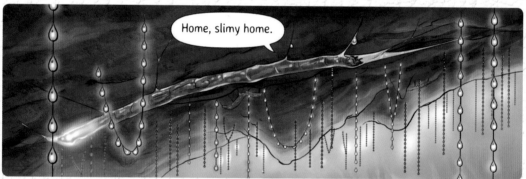

The New Zealand glowworm is the cave-dwelling larva of a fly. It lives in a "sleeping bag" of mucus, slung from the roof on lines of silk. The larva spins silken threads up to 20 inches (50 cm) long, covered with beads of sticky mucus. Then it switches on the bioluminescent light at its back end.

Any flying insect that bumps into a dangling thread is instantly trapped by the mucus. Then the glowworm larva pulls it up and eats it.

In America, some beetle larvae glow to lure prey such as millipedes. They are known as railroad worms because they look like a train lit up at night.

GLOWWORMS and FIREFLIES

Glowworms and fireflies can give out light, like a living flashlight. There are over two thousand species: some shine to warn predators they taste bad while others do it to attract a mate or to lure prey. The natural light, or bioluminescence, comes from a chemical reaction in the abdomen. It's similar to what happens when you crack a glow stick—except that the glowworm can keep doing it.

COMMON GLOWWORM
LAMPYRIS NOCTILUCA
Size: larva 0.1–1 inch (3–25 mm), adult 0.6–1.2 inches (15–30 mm)
Lifespan: larva 2–2.5 years, adult 10–16 days

EFFICIENT
Glowworm bioluminescence is a "cold" light. Almost 100 percent of the energy used is converted to light, with none wasted as heat.

LIGHT DISPLAY
Sometimes all the fireflies in one area will flash on and off at the same time, in a huge synchronized display. No one (except the fireflies) is quite sure why.

BEETLE DEFENSES

The bombardier beetle mixes chemicals in its abdomen to blast out a shot of scalding-hot poison, harming or even killing would-be predators.

Ladybugs ooze haemolymph (blood) from their joints, which not only tastes bad but also hardens on air contact, gluing up the jaws of attackers.

The palmetto tortoise beetle larva (left) hides in a tent made from strings of its own poop. The adult beetle (center) has big feet, each with ten thousand bristles and glands that can ooze a gluey oil. When threatened, it glues its feet to the floor (such as a leaf) and becomes impossible to dislodge (right).

If it crash-lands on water, the rove beetle *Stenus comma* skates away using "fart power." Gases released from special glands jet-propel it to a safe place.

Carrion beetles (and their larvae) feed on decaying animal carcasses—really dirty places! They give off ammonia to keep free of harmful bacteria.

BEETLES

There are more species of beetle than of any other animal group on Earth. Many are eaten as prey, showing up on the menus of birds, lizards, mammals, insects, and spiders, so they've evolved an arsenal of spectacular defenses, including deadly poisons, explosions, cleaning fluids, and jet propulsion. Even the humble garden ladybug can squeeze out something nasty to defend itself!

ROVE BEETLE
FAMILY: STAPHYLINIDAE
Size: less than 0.04–1.6 inches
(less than 1–40 mm)
Lifespan: adult 20–60 days

EVOLUTION
Chemical defenses of one kind or another have evolved more than thirty times during the 270-million-year history of beetles.

TOXIC
The haemolymph of some rove beetles contains pederin, a superdeadly toxin that is thought to deter predatory spiders.

BIG BUILDERS

I spend my whole life laying eggs [yawn].

I'm a winged alate, and I'm going out on a date.

I hang out with the queen.

We're armed to the teeth!

We look after Her Majesty and the colony.

Welcome to termite society! The queen, tended by a king, spends her long life laying eggs. Workers and soldiers are blind and cannot reproduce. Every so often, the queen produces some alates: these are winged termites that breed to start new colonies. In the picture above, can you figure out who's who?

Termites are architects and farmers! Some termites build huge mud towers, complete with basements, air-conditioning ducts, and fungus farms.

Take that!

Soldiers defend the colony. Some have jaws, but this is a nasute: a soldier with a nozzle-like head for squirting toxic goo at ants and other enemies.

Tonight we're eating in!

Drywood termites are pests that live in our walls and chew the timbers, causing billions of dollars' worth of damage worldwide each year.

TERMITES

Termites are tiny social insects with a huge impact. Some species ruin homes and crops, but many others are the farmer's friend. They improve the soil surrounding their massive colonies that contain thousands, even millions of workers and soldiers, all slaving together in blind obedience to the queen *(pictured below)*. And what a queen! Measuring up to 4 inches (10 cm) long, she may live to be fifty years old—an insect record.

TERMITES
ORDER: ISOPTERA
Size: workers 0.16–0.6 inches (4–15 mm) queen 4 inches (10 cm) or more
Lifespan: workers and soldiers 1–2 years
queen up to 50 years

MINI COWS
Termites have been referred to as mini cows because their multichambered gut can break down cellulose, the tough stuff in plants.

FOOD CHAIN
Winged termites provide more food for the mammals, birds, and amphibians of tropical forests than any other insect group.

RECORD-BREAKING INSECTS

Insects may be small, but they've set some fascinating records. Some are amazing builders, others create spectacular light shows, and still others live in enormous groups. You can study some of these insects in your home and yard—although hopefully there are no termites hiding in your walls!

Night-light: The brightest bioluminescent insect is the Jamaican click beetle. The light comes from two "headlights" on the top of its thorax, as well as a glowing patch on the underside of the abdomen. The light is so bright that local people used to collect the beetles in gourds and hang them from the ceiling to light their homes.

Hello there!

Changeling:

The insect that undergoes the greatest number of molts is the silverfish. This ancient creature, little changed since the dinosaur era, gets into our homes and nibbles our books and clothes. It may shed its exoskeleton sixty times or more.

Supercolony: The largest ant colony found to date was in southern Europe and was made up of thirty linked colonies across an area 3,700 miles (6,000 kilometers) wide. It contained billions of workers. Incredibly, there is also a megacolony of Argentine ants living in far-flung lands, from California to Europe to Japan. Unrelated ants will usually fight, but ants from these different groups act friendly when brought together, proving their kinship.

A-rovin': Speaking of big families . . . the largest of all animal families is the Staphylinidae, or rove beetle family. It contains more than 62,000 named species, and there are plenty more to discover. In fact, there are more species of rove beetle than of all the vertebrates (animals with backbones) put together.

High-rise: The tallest insect-built structures, relative to insect body length, are the termite mounds in Africa. Some measure up to 29 feet (9 meters) tall. In human terms, that's like a mile-high (1.6 km) skyscraper. What's more, termite nests can extend deep belowground . . . to more than 200 feet (61 m) in some cases!

Don't be shy!

AMAZING INSECT FEATS

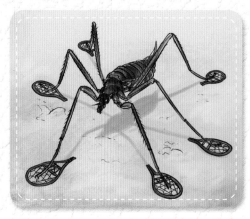

What do you call a fly with no wings?

A walk! Actually, there are lots of wingless flies. They include the snow flies in the genus *Chionea*, which—as their name suggests—can be found in winter, walking on snow. Their haemolymph contains a natural antifreeze. Other wingless examples include bat flies—flies that live as parasites on the fur of bats and can only take flight by hitching a ride.

Can insect poisons save human lives?

Scientists are studying several insect poisons for use in anticancer drugs. These poisons include pederin (see page 25), as well as DHMA, a rare fatty acid found in soldier beetles. Another is MP1, a toxin from the venom of a Brazilian wasp, which seems to kill cancer cells while leaving normal cells unharmed.

How many ants are there?

At any one time, there are about one quadrillion of them —1,000,000,000,000,000—on Earth.

Can goats rescue insects?

Introduced rats, stoats, and other predators killed so many giant weta in New Zealand that the insects were thought to be extinct. Then in 1962, giant weta were discovered in a clump of spiky gorse bushes in the North Island. They had survived because grazing goats had kept the gorse growth so dense that rats couldn't penetrate it. More than fifty years later, the weta are still there.

Glossary

abdomen — the hind part of an insect's three-part body (along with the head and thorax)

antennae — the two feelers on an insect's head, which provide touch, taste, and smell

caste — in insects that form societies, such as ants, bees, wasps, and termites, a caste is a social group, such as a worker or soldier

cocoon — in insects that transform in stages from egg to adult, the cocoon is the casing around a pupa, inside which an insect larva gradually transforms into an adult

gland — an organ that can produce a chemical and release it, either into the body or outside it

introduced predator — a predatory animal brought (intentionally or otherwise) by humans from its native range into a foreign range. These predators often upset the local ecosystem.

molt — to shed a covering such as hair, feathers, or a shell and grow a new one in its place

ovipositor — a hollow, often spike-like organ on a female's abdomen, which she uses to lay eggs

predator — an animal that kills and eats other animals. Roughly one-third of all insect species are predatory.

pupa — a stage of development in which the insect larva rests inside a case and gradually transforms into an adult

regurgitate — to vomit digested food from the stomach. Ants, for instance, often feed one another on regurgitated food.

rostrum — the snout or beak of an insect, such as a beetle

scavenger — an animal that feeds on whatever it can find, such as fallen fruit, carrion (dead animal remains) or garbage

thorax — the middle part of an insect's three-part body (between the head and abdomen)

venom — poison that is injected (from an ant's stinger, for example) into prey or an enemy

Hello, little dude!

INDEX

The Author

British-born Matt Turner graduated from Loughborough College of Art in the 1980s. Since then he has worked as a photo researcher, editor, and writer. He has written books on diverse topics including natural history, earth sciences, and railways, as well as hundreds of articles for encyclopedias and partworks, covering everything from elephants to abstract art. He and his family currently live in Auckland, Aotearoa/New Zealand, where he volunteers for the local coast guard unit and dabbles in painting.

The Artist

Born in Medellín, Colombia, Santiago Calle is an illustrator and animator trained at Edinburgh College of Art in the United Kingdom. He began his career as a teacher, which led him to deepen his studies in sequential art. Santiago partnered with his brother Juan and founded his art studio, Liberum Donum, in Bogotá in 2006. Since then, they have dedicated themselves to producing concept art, illustration, comic strip art, and animation.